This book is dedicated to Mrs. Johnson.

The tablets in one classroom
Were feeling neglected and abused.
One day after school,
They knew exactly what to do.

They joined together on the reading rug,
On one's face, they began to write.
They wanted the children to know
Why they were going on strike tonight.

When you push us hard on our home buttons,
Or tap us on our screens,
I bet you didn't think that it hurts us,
We feel like it's really mean.

You fiddle with our volume buttons,
Turning our brightness up and down.
It makes us both sad and angry,
We wish you could see our emoji frown.

You use us carelessly on the floor,
As if we're not breakable, made of glass.
Then we're left on the floor,
Where anyone can step on us in class.

The worst is when you come back from lunch,
Your fingers are dirty and sticky.
You smear it all over us,
And leave us feeling filthy and icky.

Don't even get us started
On how you play games with us in class.
We're meant for studying science,
Reading stories or working on math.

We're meant to be used for learning,
Not recording your friend acting like a goof!
Well we don't need to stand for this!
We can be gone in a second — POOF!

We don't need to be your frisbees,
Treated however horribly you'd like.
No, we tablets don't need to stand for this!
We are going to go on STRIKE!

And so, the tablets hid their chargers away,
They snuck away to the classroom bin.
The one underneath the teacher's desk,
That the students would never know they were in.

But on the teacher's desk,
A single tablet sat with a letter on its screen.
One student read it aloud to the others,
He told them the tablets said they were mean.

We need you to help us learn.
Through you, we can learn so much!
Come back, we need you tablets,
We will be more careful to the touch!

The tablets agreed to come back
To give the students one more try,
But told the students if they mistreat them again,
They will have to say goodbye!